How to Fly

(in Ten Thousand Easy Lessons)

How to Fly

(in Ten Thousand Easy Lessons)

Poetry

᠍ ᠍ ᠍ ᠍ ᠍

Barbara Kingsolver

HARPER

An Imprint of HarperCollins*Publishers*

CONTENTS

1 How to Fly

2 Pellegrinaggio

3 This Is How They Come Back to Us

4 Walking Each Other Home

5 Dancing with the Devil

6 Where It Begins

7 The Nature of Objects

1

•••••

How to Fly

How to Drink Water When There Is Wine

How to stay at this desk when the sun
is barefooting cartwheels over the grass—

How to step carefully on the path that pulls
for the fleet unfettered gait of a deer—

How to go home when the wood thrush
is promising the drunk liquid bliss of dusk—

How to resist the kiss, the body forbidden
that plucks the long vibrating string of want—

How to drink water when there is wine—

Once I knew all these brick-shaped things, took them
for the currency of survival.

Now I have lived long and I know better.

How to Have a Child

Begin on the day you decide
you are fit
to carry on.
Begin with a quailing heart
for here you stand
on the fault line.
Begin if you can at the beginning.
Begin with your mother,
with her grandfather,
the ones before him.
Think of their hands, all of them:
firm on the plow, the cradle,
the rifle butt, the razor strop;
trembling on the telegram,
the cheek of a lover,
the fact of a door.
Everything that can wreck a life
has been done before,
done to you, even. That's all
inside you now.
Half of it you won't think of.
The rest you wouldn't dream of.
Go on.

How to Cure Sweet Potatoes

Dig them after the first light frost. Lay them
down in a shallow tray like cordwood,
like orphans in a dresser drawer. Cover them
with damp towels. Bring up the heat. In a
closet or spare room, you'll want it hotter
than the worst summer day you remember
and that humid. A week of this will thicken
their skins, make them last for months
in your cellar, and turn all their starch to sugar.

Bear in mind this is not a cure for anything
that was wrong with the sweet potato
that meant to be starchy, thanks, the better
to weather a winter in cold clay, then lean on its toes
and throw out reckless tendrils into one more spring.

Bear in mind also the ways that you were once
induced to last through the sermon, the meal,
the insufferable adult conversation, all the times
you wanted to be starchy but were made to be sweet.

Recall this surrender when you sit down to eat them.
Consider the direction of your grace.

How to Shear a Sheep

Walk to the barn
before dawn.
Take off your clothes.
Cast everything
on the ground:
your nylon jacket,
wool socks, and all.
Throw away
the cutting tools,
the shears that bite
like teeth at the skin
when hooves flail
and your elbow
comes up hard
under a panting throat:
no more of that.
Sing to them instead.
Stand naked
in the morning
with your entreaty.
Ask them to come,
lay down their wool
for love.
That should work.
It doesn't.

How to Fly (in Ten Thousand Easy Lessons)

Behold your body as water
and mineral worth, the selfsame
water that soon (from a tree's
way of thinking, *soon*) will be
lifted through the elevator hearts
of a forest, returned to the sun
in a leaf-eyed gaze. And the rest!
All wordless leavings, the perfect
bonewhite ash of you: light
as snowflakes, falling on updrafts
toward the unbodied breath of a bird.

Behold your elements reassembled
as pieces of sky, ascending
without regret, for you've been lucky
enough. Fallen for the last time into
a slump, the wrong crowd, love.
You've made the best deal.
You summitted the mountain
or you didn't. Anything left undone
you can slip like a cloth bag of marbles
into the hands of a child
who will be none the wiser.

Imagine your joy on rising.
Repeat as necessary.

How to Give Thanks for a Broken Leg

Thank your stars that at least your bones
know how to knit, two sticks at work:
tibia, fibula, ribbed scarf as long as a winter.
The mindless tasks a body learns when it must.

Praise your claw-foot tub. Tie a sheet around its belly
like a saddle on a pig, to hammock your dry-docked
limb while the rest of you steeps. Sunk deep
in hot water up to your chin, dream of the troubles
you had, when trouble was still yours to make.
The doctor says eight weeks. Spend seven here.

Be glad for your cast that draws children with
permanent markers, like vandals and their graffiti
to the blighted parts of town. They mark out
their loves and territories, and you, the benevolent
mayor, will wear these concerns in public,
then throw them away when your term is up.

Concede your debt to life's grammar, even as
it nailed you in one fell stroke from subject to object.
Praise the helping verbs, family hands that feed;
the surgical modifiers that pin you from shattered
to fixed to mended. Praise the careless syntax
of a life where, through steady misuse, a noun
grows feet: it turtles and outfoxes and one day,
with no one watching, steps out as a brand-new verb.

How to Survive This

O misery. Imperfect
universe of days stretched out
ahead, the string of pearls
and drops of venom on the web,
losses of heart, of life
and limb, news of the worst:

Remind me again
the day will come
when I look back amazed
at the waste of sorry salt
when I had no more than *this*
to cry about.

Now I lay me down.
I'm not there yet.

How to Do Absolutely Nothing

Rent a house near the beach, or a cabin
but: Do not take your walking shoes.
Don't take any clothes you'd wear
anyplace anyone would see you.
Don't take your rechargeables.
Take Scrabble if you have to,
but not a dictionary and no
pencils for keeping score.
Don't take a cookbook
or anything to cook.
A fishing pole, ok
but not the line,
hook, sinker,
leave it all.
Find out
what's
left.

How to Lose That Stubborn Weight

Follow this simple program:
Examine your elbow, the small bones
in your wrist. Kiss what you can.
Gather up all the magazines
and catalogues in your house—those
hungry girls in expensive clothes.
Put them all inside your refrigerator.
Next, your streaming videos and
discreetly altered friends: balance these
in a pile on your bathroom scale.
Leave them there for sixteen weeks.
See how the weight melts away
from the craven core. Listen,
all God's children got this yearn
and half of them wish they could look
just about like you do now. And so
will you, if you ever get to be ninety.
That photo that set you off today?
How you'll wish you'd taken more,
back when your skin still held
the shape of a lusty animal you forgot
to love, wish you'd hung mirrors
on all your walls and halls and
oh hell, the fat blue indifferent sky
in praise of this body you had one time
when everything still worked.

How to Get a Divorce

Fight for these things:
>One phone call to your mother-in-law.
>The credit you deserve, because

sacrifice for love is a cozy hearth, or a spark
that burns down the house. It's all in the timing.
>The flimsy relics of childhood, yours.
>The car you could talk to.
>The tools you learned to live by.
>Your children intact, blessed by your diplomacy,

a language of words you will chisel out of ice.
No work you've ever done will cost you more,
or purchase more.

Don't fight for these:
>The car that's not paid for.
>Every gift you pretended to like.

Take one object treasured by your spouse,
something small that won't be missed:
>Smash it with a rock.
>Bury the remains in the backyard.
>Bear the pall however. It's your party.
>By the powers vested in hearsay,
>your marriage is now oil and water.

Some of your friends will choose to drink the oil.

These you have to give up:
>Collected shells and pressed flowers.
>The eyes that knew your body
>when it was still perfect. Everything must go.
>Don't throw it in the Grand Canyon. Seal it all

in a box with packing tape, shoved to the back of a closet.

Years from now, when some passion brings new order
to your household, you will open this box. Find inside:
      Music you've since gone looking for.
      Wedding photos, two sweet kids with comical hair.
      A ring for your daughter, prop for the story
      she's had to rewrite alone.
      Your one-time self in a rummage of lost and found.

Quietly set it all out on a shelf in plain sight
      because, like rain and gravity, these things
      are right, and flattening, and dearly necessary,
      and inasmuch as they're anyone's,
they're yours.

How to Be Married

Think of rain: the gathering sheer fall
on a quaking plain. Like a kiss,
the long slake. Here we stand
in blissful drench. It only falls;
no calling it back from here.
River infinite, grinding belly on bedrock,
paring the plain to a canyon,
changing the shape of the world.
Love is no granite boulder, praised
for its size. It's the water that parts
around it, moving mountains.
Nothing new, a marriage. This union
is as old as it gets: ocean floor,
the wave and shore that can't be still
and can't come apart. Think of
blue-gray horizons, heavy-lidded.
Don't rule out surprising possibilities.
An ocean can rise up whole
into the firmament, given eternity.
No going back from today.
Water flows downhill and still
we are here, new as naked children
standing in the cool precipitous fall: think of rain.

How to Knit a Sweater (a Realist's Prayer)

O Lord
(whether male, female,
animate, all-knowing,
unreasonable or just
whether or not),
we are practical people
who hedge our bets.
As I hold my loved ones
this day in my thoughts,
meditating on our hopes
and wild adversities,
I also hold a skein
of good wool,
needles that click like
rosary beads working
through Hail Marys
of knit and purl.
By involving fiber
in my invocation
of divinity,
I feel assured
of a fairly positive outcome.

How to Love Your Neighbor

All of them. Not just the morning shoppers,
the man who walks his chortling dog, the couples
with strawberry children. These are the given.

Announce your rebel kindness in letters painted
much too large on the back of your jacket. Children
will stare, dogs bark. Doors bolt. Anyway, walk.

Your shoes will wear out, and then your knees.
You will feel the cold's every angle, the want of rain,
a drought of blessings. Your vanished face.

Close by, behind dust-colored curtains, a woman
wrapping her hijab—girding herself for the street
of this day—will call to her husband: *Come see.*

These two will kneel at their window.
Mercy wears lightning bolts on her shoulder. Threads
of fire in her white hair. The face of the sun.

How to Be Hopeful

Look, you might as well know,
this device is going to take endless repair:
rubber cement, rubber bands, tapioca,
the square of the hypotenuse,
nineteenth-century novels, sunrise—
any of these could be useful. Also feathers.
The ignition is tricky. Sometimes
you have to stand on an incline
where things look possible. Or a line
you drew yourself. Or the grocery line,
making faces at a toddler, secretly,
over his mother's shoulder.
You may have to pop the clutch
and run past the evidence. Past everyone
who is praying for you. Passing
all previous records is ok, or passing
strange. Just not passing it up.
Or park it and fly by the seat of your pants.
With nothing in the bank, you will
still want to take the express. Tiptoe
past the dogs of the apocalypse
asleep in the shade of your future.
Pay at the window. You'll be surprised:
you can pass off hope like a bad check.
You still have time, that's the thing.
To make it good.

2

⁕⁕⁕⁕⁕

Pellegrinaggio

I. Pellegrinaggio

At the end of the long bowling alley lane
of a transatlantic flight, we crash and topple
like pins in the back of a Roman taxi.
Split or spare, hard to say what we are but
family, piled across one another: husband
and wife, our two daughters, his mother
Giovanna who has waited eighty years
to see what she's made of.

Her parents, flung out from here like messages
in bottles, washed up on a new shore and grew
together. Grew celery for the Americans. Grew this
daughter who walked to school, sewed a new
cut of skirt, and became the small interpreter
for a family. They took her at her word but stamped
a map called *home* on a life she believed would end
before she could ever come here to find it.

What other gift could we give her? But now our taxi
crawls like a green bottlefly through the ear canals
of a city, it is half-past something I can't stand
one more minute of, and I wonder what we were
thinking. We all might die before we find a place
to lie in this bed we've made for her. Beside me
she sits upright, mast of our log-pile ship in this bottle.
Made of everything that has brought us this far.

II. The Roman Circus

Navigating the tram:
Do not mount the car without a ticket.
Your ticket must be purchased
within the car.

Exchanging traveler's checks:
Go to the Spanish Steps! everyone agrees, for there
(and nowhere else) officials will accept our deficient
currency and throw baskets of money upon us.

The Spanish Steps:
Excuse the inconvenience as
the American Express is closed.

The Pantheon:
Do not doubt that a yogurt-flavored gelato
could be unparalleled in civilized human experience.
Or the fig, as a close second.

Trevi Fountain:
Elbow yourself into the crowd
of travelers throwing coins
to guarantee another journey here, more elbows,
more chances, one more coin.

III. On the Piazza

Through the scent of grilled fish
a tarantella rises from the boy
in tattered jeans but startling shoes—
formal, black, perfectly polished—
who plays his violin as if this
teeming plaza were Carnegie Hall
and his shoes, in that case, correct.
We drink Chianti and keep an eye
on the sweet-talking boys who cruise
like sleek reef fish, slip bracelets
onto our daughters' pretty wrists:
One euro, or your phone number.
Jugglers stab at the darkness
with flaming knives or the modern
electric equivalent. But the one who's
got me is the tall masked pharaoh
in a gold drape who stands
immobile on a box, hour upon
hour, his statuesque illusion
a frozen, untouched island
in the churning human torrent,
except for his silent, folded bow
when a coin is dropped at his feet.
Later, relief arrives. The pharaoh
wriggles free of his gilded cocoon—
the metamorphosis—and his brother
crawls in to take his shift. I imagine
their small apartment shared with
other immigrants from an African
village of emptied-out fields,
the intimacy of these two brothers
living mostly just the one life now
on Piazza Navona inside a golden sheet.

IV. Into the Abruzzo

Vomipeligna, the kids will later
name this. Car pulled over
onto the grassy verge of a much-too-
winding road, the pale among us helping
the ones beyond it. How quickly
a roving family may find togetherness.

We are trying to find our way back
to the motherland. For air I wander into
a field and find wild peonies blooming.
Dancing, madly fragrant. Who knew
the portly bouquets of Memorial Days
hailed from such winsome hay-haired kin?

Here to remind me of graveyards
and surprising sites of origin.
A mountain that holds us to its secrets.
These feral granite ranges gave the world
children, the mother of my mother-in-law,
her son, our family, and peonies.

V. In Torricella, Finding Her Mother's House

Here is the church. Mamma went
every day, not just to pray but to sing.
The boys dropped spiders on the girls
from the balcony. One of the boys, she liked.
Here is the house beside the church
where the lawyer lived. He was rich.
Mamma came every morning
to help the lawyer's wife dress
and comb her long hair, to earn a coin.
Six doors down, here is the house
where she lived. Where her papa died.
Where they had nothing. Out of this door
they went, she and her sister as children.
They stood on this step to say goodbye.
A stagecoach to Naples, from there a ship,
to live with the cousin in Denver who
had a tavern. Girls could work there.
They didn't know the cousin. Here is
the graveyard where she saw her papa
buried, the doorstep where she kissed
the mamma she would never see again.
Over the ocean to make her way,
it started here.
                    Look at this view.
Why did she never tell me it was
beautiful here? Never speak of so much,
so much she left behind.

VI. Circumnavigating Torricella Peligna

Giovanna wants to know
what there is to know about
this mountain. Anything her mother
might have seen if she walked
downhill. Expecting not a lot, we
drive through towns, each smaller
than the one before. A church,
a fountain. The town band on
the square, all the young faces
behind the bright blossoming bells
of their instruments, the pollen
drift of their music. The *pozzo*
where cold water wells up
from the stone heart of the land.
A trattoria, a waiter who somehow
sees everything, *famiglia*. Asks
younger guests to move so she
will have the best view. Tells our
girls their *nonna* is an encyclopedia.
They should read her every day.
We watch clouds tease like a veil
across the forested bluffs, but she is
watching the mountain, her true north.

VII. Pompeii

It's terrible, but we want to know
all about the unfortunates caught flat
when the mountain blew. We've read the
firsthand account by Pliny the Younger,
imagined the bay clogged with pumice,
the screamers running around with
pillows clasped to their heads. Now
in the streets of their city we step high
on great stone crosswalks designed
for simultaneous passage of wagon wheels,
pedestrians, and sewage. We admire
the murals in their villas (in vogue then: red,
and Egypt). Eager voyeurs, we drink it in
like those doomed souls lined up
at the taverns with their jugs. We visit
the brothel and then the stadium with
perfect acoustics that make us sing.
Saved for last, the Garden of Fugitives,
where mothers clung to their children
behind the high wall, clawing for escape.
Fossilized on their upturned faces we see
the belief that anyone would recognize:
in one more minute we will breathe again.
As people do, we've come looking
for proof that the dead of the past were just
like us. And grow quiet, having found it.

VIII. At the Top of Mount Vesuvius

The view from here—
down flower-bronzed slopes
to the apron of cities from Naples
to Sorrento—is one long allowance
of habitation along the bay.

How many lives have hugged this sea,
how many eyes lifted to this crater
wondering when she might throw
her next fit of boiling lava?
Puddled mounds like cow dung

reveal themselves to be buried towns.
A fringe of steam leaks from the crater's
smile. Her breath has notes of sulfur.
But underneath this fine flat pledge of sky
the sea is calm. The blood-red roofs.

Even the newest houses, bone-colored,
and the many more under construction.
The view from here reaches backward
into centuries; from down there forward only
as far as half-past tomorrow.

IX. Swimming in the Bay of Naples

You float. I am not kidding.
Your own shocking toes rise up
to let you know. This is not

like the cloying dark ponds of
childhood, or the college pool
where my lank leaden frame
angled down and down beneath
the bluster of the swimming
instructor who insisted I would
float if I just applied myself.

How could I know? I had only
to acquire an Italian family
and follow it here to this sweetly
salted sea like a fat featherbed
where a body can lie in repose
considering the successes
of civilized people. Never mind

what's below, the real estate
of old shipwrecks. I will stay

up here. Now that I know the secret.

X. On the Train to Sicily

In a family compartment we take the long
ride south, down the coast and across the channel
to the *patria* of her father. She is so tired.
We've lifted her onto the sill of this urbane clatter,
tucked ourselves in a cupboard of relative
peace, but now her small frame finds no resting
place on the great square seats. We offer
pillows, sips of water. She only says, *Don't worry*.

Panoramas pass in dramatic excess: castles,
vineyards, splendidly pointed mountains cloaked
in olive trees. We feel abashed for these
wonders, but worry that we've dragged her bones
through too many stations of this cross.
The unstoppable rhythm of filial love pulls us on
and on along its track. South of Cetraro
our cupboard is invaded: a girl. Deep blue hair

drawn low across her brow like a wartime
blackout curtain. Inked with skulls and crossbones
to her knuckles, dark eyes resting loose
on the air overhead. She ignores us.
We rock in a silent tedium of mutual discomfort,
willing this suddenly scrambled nest into something
whole again, when the ring of her mobile
snaps her into focus, window flung wide: *Ciao, Mamma!*

XI. Monreale

My grandmother came here just once.
People rarely traveled in those days,

she tells us, as we navigate the twisting
approach, steering wheel arm over elbow,
not far outside Palermo but what a road.

She spoke of it for the rest of her life.
She had never seen anything like it.

Afterward we grow talkative with
our marvel at the cathedral, its golden
mosaics and honeycombed ceiling,
chatter about the different kinds of
beauty, our good luck at seeing
a wedding party arrive, that dress
of hers. The white Rolls-Royce
parked in front! Our marvel wanders.
Giovanna in the back seat closes her eyes:

I'm going to be quiet now
and think about my grandmother.

XII. Lemon-Orchard Blue

The language has its words
for blue—*azzurro, blu, ciano*—
and it could use some more.
Tranquil sea, tormented sea,
shallow and deep, stormy but stippled
with light, a blue where anything
could be hiding behind an alibi
of sepia ink. And this does not begin
to address the sky: glazed
like a Moorish tile, or furtive
as a memory of Vesuvius.
Innocent as a twenty-cent postcard.
These are the sturdy blues
that stand in line for an eye to call out.

Others wait behind them: the blue,
for instance, that was always here
stretched tight as a laundered sheet
above the orchard where a point-eared dog
stalks his lizard and the lemon trees
bend their arms, whitewashed to the elbow,
pushing flat bouquets of leaves
against heaven, the wheeling swallows,
and one season's ration of cloud.

XIII. The Road to Erice Is Paved with Intentions

My mother-in-law, as she puts it, has intentions.
Advice from a priest to carry a heart
past unbearable losses, a husband and daughter,
and strike its path through one more day:
Get up and make intentions.
I intend to call a friend on the phone.
I intend to notice the flowers in the yard.

It cannot be easy to be this old, with a heart
tugged by loss and a family's interventions
across the stones of Sicily. But on we go, I declare
the plan for our day: we will drive to Erice.
Picture us up there gazing down at the water,
across the blue southern seas. If the day
is fine, I intend for us to see all the way to Rome.

Erice has other intentions, remains a hard
medieval gleam on the mountaintop—shaved
white scoop of vanilla ice on a tall volcanic cone.
It melts as we lurch and falter up the winding trace
where so many men try to stop us. First, a scare
with a flagman, next the funicular man, and then
the carabinieri. But I am intent: we slip by.

At a roadblock, we are forced to park the car.
Boldly I link my arm through hers and declare
to all men gathered there, "I've brought her
this far. We are going to walk to Erice." They wave
and waggle their heads as if we are Verdi's demented
foreign witches. But she and I with heads held high
march past their barricade. And that is when

they start screaming, *"Una gara!"* With the rising roar
it dawns: *gara*, garage, holy mother, *an auto race*.
Flung to the ditch, our hearts surpassing all known
limits, the steel-flanked beasts shrieking by
in their pitched stampede, we had our shave,
my resolute mother-in-law and I, so close. To Erice.
Our headstones might read: These ladies had intentions.

XIV. Palermo

La nonna cammina, she walks
through the hectoring fish-scale
cobble of the street market.
We are here to find her father
who cast off from this rocky island
a hundred years ago, hoping
to join his father on a Rocky
Mountain railroad crew, arriving
just in time for the burial cairn
of stones piled up beside the half-
laid track. Orphaned at twelve
in a roughneck camp, illiterate,
perseverant as a stone himself,
he labored the rest of his days
to bring what remained of his clan
to a new world. What could he
have left behind? No family hearth
or tilled valley; Palermo was
a village then, has spent the years
churning up fields and cottages,
growing tall buildings, and nothing,
maybe, is here for us to find—no knot
for a daughter to grasp at the end
of the long rope of this pilgrimage.

Our family threads its way through
brine-tinged morning light, a gloss
of eggplants racked like billiards,
long-armed men flaying anchovies
with the efficiency of seabirds. I follow
my husband, suddenly stirred by
the sight of his hand on her elbow,
steering his little rowboat of a mother

through this bounding main. Our
days alfresco have darkened his skin.
He could be brother to any of these
hawkers of Trapani salt or sardines.
Time and again she makes him stop:
These olives were Papa's favorite. These
fig garlands we always had at Christmas.
She left this language behind at six—
firmly, like a hangdog pet that
followed her to the schoolroom
door—but now the words turn up
like found pennies under her tongue:
Arancini, melanzana. Oh, zucca lunga!
Impossibly long green squashes,
thin as a schoolgirl's arm. *He grew*
these in Colorado from Sicilian seeds—
she remembers this, and the tendrils
he clipped each morning from the
ends of vines that always grew back,
brought in like bouquets for his
freshly minted American daughters.
Mamma boiled those with salt and
olive oil, and that was breakfast.

At a butcher's stall we all pause
to gaze at ovals of glistening flesh
piled up like white creek stones.
My mother-in-law has no word,
so I ask, *Che cosè?* The butcher
winks at mothers and daughters,
points to the one man among us:
They are the things that he has.
We smile, embarrassed, and not

because we surely knew. Paternity
is the rope with no knot at its end,
the burial cairn, the garden seed,
the rigged mast of every ship
that had to sail. What's left behind
thrusts forward. Potent *Italia*.

3

•••••

This Is How They Come Back to Us

Burying Ground

This cemetery is full of too much living,
leaves of grass exhaling
under our polished shoes,

trees too burnished
with copperplate autumn,
a sky too elated today

to revoke a touch our skin
remembers as kin, to cast a voice still in
our ears into the hushed ground,

and this air, too much like breath,
the children too wonder-struck with strange
fortune in this ranging throng

of cousins, their black skirts twirling
like pinwheels over the stony lawn, bouquets
of dark flowers hurled into sunshine.

Hearts full afraid of the asking price.
Too much for this day
if this is the end of the world.

This Is How They Come Back to Us

—For A. R. Henry, 1898–1970

I think of my grandfather Henry
with a claw hammer in his hand,
untroubled by the missing tip of
one finger, though it worries me.
I think of him spooning sugar on a
slice of tomato, the white mound
melting clear. Eating it for dessert.
I think of the teeth that are not his
teeth, slid forward into a bear smile
to frighten me, and then his laughter
that takes it all back, tooth and bear.
I think of him asleep in a chair, arms
crossed, as I have seen men in coffins.
I think of him scaling the college steps
to meet my grandmother, unashamed
to take off his hat and show the white
stripe above the burnished brow, the
face of a man who works in the sun.
I think of him young with still-perfect
hands lifting a daughter onto a pony,
teaching this girl to ride bareback over
the Fox Creek hills. She is my mother,
I am not alive, and yet I can see these
things because my grandfather Henry
is dead. All these parts of his life are
equal now, the end and the beginning.

Passing Death

—For JoEllen Hopp Petri, 1959–2006

For her children, this gradual dying
is like the tests at school that leave no one behind:
death mastered in small increments.
Last summer they lost her laugh,
the surprise of a marshmallow sandwich,
jokes while she folded laundry,
a sheet furled around the make-believe bride.
By then we knew she wouldn't see their weddings.

In the fall they learned to walk the dog without her.
Running is lost before walking,
laughter before smiling, hope before fear.
The tumor presses each of these
from her mind like slick melon seeds
squeezed out of a fist until nothing is left
but the sticky-sweet cling of living.
A late-afternoon light touches her sleeves

but not her face as we sit at the table, unspeaking,
dredging prospects without bearing.
The bravelings whirl past us chasing the dog,
casting their sandwiches upon the furniture.
Their household has lost the word *no*.
When we bury her, what will be left for them
to cry over? Spilled milk, indelible stain.
One last ounce of a mother drained away.

The Visitation

—*For Ralph Hopp, 1922–2001*

The father, who knew how to fight
every illness and win, a surgeon
who reattached fingers and even noses,
defying all the laws of tragedy we knew,
now rests
                    with unease in his chair.
We've brought words
for repairing the terms of his valor,
but words are not his tools.

We are guards at a pillaged vault,
already dismissed from our day and
night shifts but lingering
anyway in the quiet living
room where he hosts
                    Cancer as his guest.
The two of them are not speaking.
He is angry.
It can't be helped.

Long Division

—For Dante Salvatierra, 1972–2015

According to the rules you stand alone,
facing off against the larger number elbowed
into its bracket: divide and conquer. But you

would throw the bracket open, walk right in,
persuading all those present to dance,
leading them outside under trees to study
on the grass of a child's better nature. You

would always rather add than subtract;
would carry the one, on your shoulders if need be:
the bully-worn muggle with untied shoelaces,
the latchkey kids who pick every lock and find
their true home. They'd follow you anywhere. You

should see all these people who used to be
third graders, gathered here to wish for one last
thing, for the life of you. But this train has been
coming for us all, so long. You stashed your
absolute values in a river of children that runs
to the sea, runs for good. Now take away one, you.

The remainder looks impossible. How to begin
the long division: these days ahead, all broken apart?
Now we set our shoes to the pavement of living.
Now you pass through the brick wall of this station
to enter the autumn air of a better nature. You

altogether, one hundred percent.

My Great-Grandmother's Plate

—For Lillie Auxier, 1881–1965

New Year's morning, standing
at the sink watching new snow drift,
I cosset a hope that this weather might
persist, bundling a household
of family into one more day as mine
before the world calls us out again.

It whitens the woods while I weather
a washing-up from last night's happy ending:
the grass-stemmed goblets, dorsal spines
of underwater forks, and last, the white
china platter with lattice edges, a gift
to my great-grandmother for her wedding.

I use this plate because I want to know
how it might make me one with her, my hands
slipped into hers like a pair of gloves as I lift
and admire its fragile rim, sharing our standing
as householders, dutiful washers of porcelain.
But instead, a presence from behind me takes

my shoulders, and I feel her dread of a snow
like this for her new husband's sake,
a man called out to cattle in any weather;
feel her brooding on a shuttered-up morning
for its cost in coal. This delicate wedding
gift might plague her for the note her mother

will be expecting soon, along with other
good news. A washing-up left for the morning
would not have been her liberty. My hands
may reach but cannot share this porcelain gift:
the newest stake of her household,
the oldest one in mine.

Thank-You Note for a Quilt

—For Neta Webb Findley, 1920–2018

Your stitches still remind me of beans in May:
their bowed heads emerging in perfect rows.

Or blackberry canes that arch and fall,
marching across the hayfield between my house

and yours, quietly stitching our neighborhood
into one grassy quilt for the crows to name.

When you were a child planting lilacs here
with your mother, did you imagine the same

honeyed scent, eighty years later, waking
someone like me in this house, or that we

would sit on this porch stitching and binding
together, or that you would finally show me

how to fall in love with the time on my hands,
to plant flowers to outlive me? This quilt

is more than one of your winters, a falling-leaves
pattern passed down. It is the bed I am still

making up under blackberry winters come and
gone. The grace of passing over, passing on.

My Mother's Last Forty Minutes

—For Virginia Henry Kingsolver, 1929–2013

At three in the afternoon we heard the death rattle,
sound of a throat that can't clear itself anymore.
This was the cue for another drop of morphine, or not,
according to a nurse's advice my sister and I tried to
reconstruct, as earnestly as we used to kneel together
to build our fairy houses of tree bark and moss. We'd
slept almost not at all for a week, and between us now
constructed no clear game plan on the morphine.

Really, *death rattle* was all I kept thinking. As if
the den of this ranch house smelling of sickroom
and dust, with its flotsam of empty Kleenex boxes,
its rented hospital bed and oxygen machine, its frugal
postwar windows and chronic gloom, had received
a surprise visitor and it was Charles Dickens.

> *May I say that life is filled with instructions
> we just don't believe we are ever going to need?*

My father announced he had checks to deposit, so
was going to the bank. My sister and I locked eyes,
the old familiar rope of the drowning child. She
suggested to him that he might regret his timing.
I followed him outside. This is my family job, to say
the ungentle thing. Taking it for the team. I yelled
at him briefly. Then apologized. We were none of us
quite in our minds and anyway, who was I to judge?

As far as I knew he hadn't spent a night or a day
away from my mother in something like half
a century, while I was off living my own merry life,
had merely put it on hold for a couple of weeks

to come and help out with the dying-at-home-
with-no-hired-help request.

                    *Again I'll step out
of that room to warn the unwitting: it's a big ask.*

My father came back inside. The three of us
sat in chairs arranged like planets around our sun.
She hadn't spoken in days, or opened her eyes,
yet her gravity held us. Though not completely.
I'd noticed Dad now shifting his gaze, staring in
love and wonder at the 12×14 portrait of my mother
gorgeously veiled as a twenty-year-old bride, which
he'd set on the mantel to pretty up this departure.

The rain picked up. This storm was something else,
some wild stampede on the roof of my childhood
home. But she seemed shipshape, fresh cotton gown,
no furrows of pain on the pale crepe of her brow.
I took my phone out to the sunporch to update our
brother. I'd barely spoken when a bolt of lightning
struck the house. Zipped right down a metal duct
an arm's reach away from me. I dropped the phone.

Took a moment. My heart, still beating.
The house, utterly silent. The electricity had gone
out, which made things seem peaceful.
I remembered oxygen. That she would suffocate.
I hurried back to the den where my sister and I
in treble octaves discussed the emergency
backups. Then noticed our mother was breathing
on her own. She hadn't done this since last winter.

Around half-past, a shuddering little house-quake
brought the power back on. We breathed.
My mother's pulse-oxygen, measured by a device
pinched on her finger—a number we watched
like the basketball scores, like the polls before
an election—had plunged to the failure zone. Now
with machine assist she rallied back into the nineties.
Dean's List. All her life, that's where she liked to be.

This might be the moment to step one last time
from the bedside to mention that while we spoke kindly,
mostly, my mother and I did not love one another.
Ever, not even when I was a baby—as I've lately learned
from letters she wrote her friend from a cold plywood
house in Annapolis where I crawled up her legs and
drove her nuts, where she begged my two-year-old brother
to look after me, wished Dad would come home
from the navy and they could zoom away from us
in their aquamarine Chevrolet.

When women are instructed to bear children,
we don't think of such possibilities.
That we are on our own here. There is no Dean's List.

The blessing is that later, in better times, she had
another daughter. I cherished my sister too; it's no fault
of hers that lightning only strikes once. I would be
the unspeakable first failure that stuck in my mother's
throat, the child who would never be gentled,
or allowed to touch her good things, or even allowed to
take her to lunch, but could take the rap, the bad daughter.

However I might hold myself to the goods of my own life,
the too-many lovers, the eventual sweet husband,
the daughters more necessary to me than my two eyes,
none of this could alter the daughter I was.
But for these last weeks—

                          —but for these last weeks
while I spoon-fed my mother and crushed pain
medicine into liquid drops on her tongue,
did things too intimate to say—the bathing
and changing she once did for me, that trapped
her so terribly—through all these labors she
seemed to be sleeping but sometimes unexpectedly
gripped my hand, and did not zoom away.

She left on her own recognizance. No final
confessions, still the untroubled brow, the oxygen
thanklessly pumping away. The rattle went quiet.
The pulse-ox fell to zero. At some point the thunder
had ceased, the storm passed over. I have
no recollection of a house filled with so much light.
The trees outside, so bright with rain. So much depends.
Here begins my life as no one's bad daughter.

4

·····

Walking Each Other Home

By the Roots

Crouched in the garden
knees to elbows, fists to the earth,
wrenching weedy orchard grass
from the mud-soaked roots
of my tendered corn,
ripping the soil that feeds me,
feeling its outrage, I am
all of a moment tearing out
the hair of the world. Memory runs
through me like hot water: My brother

is nine. I am seven, loyal as oxygen
but still near enough his size
that our fights want to go
to the death. Our parents
reflect, too late, on the charms
of the only child. We two
are hell-bent, knees burnt raw
by the grass, our fists to earth,
my knuckles twined in his hair
cannot stop pulling: dear God

the terror in that helpless crave for
wounding the one you couldn't live without.

My First Derby Party

He says I am old enough now to stop hating horses.
This Kentucky friend, youngest of eight, who started
school in shoes that had already been to first grade
twice. I was luckier, newly shod at each summer's end.

For the purchase we always drove to Lexington, past
all the mansions, fists tucked into my sweaty armpits,
scowling from the back seat at the training center
where horses had a swimming pool all their own.

Important horses, according to my mother. No child
in our county, white nor brown nor gritty from setting
tobacco, was important enough for a swimming pool.
We had the Licking River and snapping turtles.

How I despised those rich foals tossing their manes,
running the length of a birthright on green bluegrass.
Our schoolyard was gravel. We brought it home when
scrapes with our authorities embedded it in our knees.

Some girls dreamed of currycombs and power
clenched between their thighs, had secret names
for the thoroughbreds they'd have one day. Not me.
I looked up *blueblood*, connected blood and grass.

On school day mornings, on Derby Day at the starting
gate, we sang one song. Children with tobacco-stained
hands, Louisville ladies in fancy hats: we all stood
together to reconcile ourselves to the state of our birth.

And now the friend who's traveled these same miles
with me is having a Derby Party. For our juleps
I pick mint from my arid garden, where I've tried
for years to cultivate the greenness of Kentucky.

The sun shines bright. I squint at the sky, consider
how far I've run without bloodline or contract.
We will sing one song for my Old Kentucky Home,
revising the words as needed. *Weep no more, my lady.*

We gather to watch the run for the roses on television
at five thirty sharp, tape-delayed to erase the time
we've lost. Shoulder to shoulder we watch the shining
muscle-bound haunches straining under the whip.

It ends with a great gold cup in the owner's hands,
a victor with neck bent low by roses he can't even eat,
our glasses raised: freeborn, field-stained, I wonder
at my old envy for the well-shod mansion slave.

Snow Day

The blizzard came and went last night as we slept.

The woods were first to wake up
as their own black-and-white photograph.

Next a rabbit: revealed
as the history of its many
indecisions along the lane.

Black ponies on the hill:
round-bellied shadows of creatures
that stood just yesterday
in their own breakfast.

The pasture: a toboggan slope.
Children who wait like fence posts,
on other days, for the school bus
now howl their demon love for speed,
calling me to join them.

Nothing is what it was.
The mailbox sports a white toupee,
compensating for a certain
internal emptiness.
The mail won't come today.
All professions called on account of weather.

Every identity canceled. I have no choice
but to set down these words,
wrap my long limbs in the cloak
of a perfect disguise,
walk down the lane,
steal into life as a ten-year-old
leaving footprints: traces of my escape.

Six Women Swimming Naked in the Ocean

An even dozen, as it happens,
changeable as the lunar egg
and milky like that, breasts
that have waxed and waned
answering the tides and tugs that
rule the world: men and children.

These bosoms have heaved
with passion and impatience,
but here in the midnight ocean
they just float
like jellyfish. Lifebuoys. Bottles
flung out with no message inside.

We tumble and crash like so much
sandy laundry, sing out names,
keep an eye on each other
by means of our headlamps,
twelve shiny melons. We
have been called so many things,

have come from so many places.
Earlier in the beach house we were all
such different people—modest, illustrious,
or provisional—forgetting we had this
standard equipment to bind us.
And once unbound, to carry us away.

Courtship Dance on Playa Luria

The tourists' bikinis touch down like witless butterflies
trying to suck nectar from the blazing sand
while the feet of the blanket vendors trudge across it
on thick black soles they have cannily cut from tires.

Blankets she has seen. But never this one on his shoulder,
woven color on color, luminous birds. Nuptial plumage.

He sees her looking.

Gazing across the field of torpid sleepers
into her eyes, he squares himself against blue sea,
snaps out his arms, opening wide the blanket.

                    She glances away.

Too late, he's caught her. Now with every turn
of her head he throws open the feathered wings again,
dares her to imagine these wild colors in her bed.

          She inhales through pursed lips:
¿Cuánto es?
          His mouthed response:
                    Treinta y cinco.

Too much: she tosses her head to the side.
          He counters:
                    For you only thirty.

She looks away. Then back.
          Barely moving her lips, offers fifteen.

He hangs his head, colorful feathers offended.

She shrugs, reaches into her bag where all he asks
and more is hiding, pulls out a book instead,
inciting his fevered passion:

> *For you, twenty-five!*
> *For you, I am prepared to lose everything.*

She opens the book, shows him
her doubtful profile, the shape of his loss.

Suddenly there is motion. Through one narrowed eye
she watches the sunburned matron, flagging spandex,
owl-eyed shades, swooping out on scalded feet
toward her suitor. The gray curls nod: *Thirty-five only!*

Clutching her gravid bag, the wallet extracted,
sincerity takes all. This dance is done.

I was the one. For whom he would lose everything:
left to imagine even now those colors on my bed
as he slips the bills in his pocket and leaves me forever.

Will

Who will peel these red hearts,
Roma, San Marzano,
that have to be slipped
by the hundreds from their skins?
I will, she says. My mother-in-law is
ninety, her bones the slimmest threads

to stitch a body heels to skull, a tenuous
seam of spine. The everyday apron
that swaddles my curves
hangs from her neck toward the floor
like a living-room drape. Here
in my kitchen, the little red hen: I will.

The heartless tomato massif
looms in bowls and colanders.
As reliable as geology and erosion:
the will of her hands, the motion
of mountains, the ocean of marinara
in our cauldron. She is rock, and I am

weather, dancing from stove to pantry and
back, conducting our creation with my wand
of steel spoon, reading our crystal ball
of steamed canning jars where our family
secrets of thyme and salt will meld with
the elements of one more growing season.

Time slips away from us, comes back: I see
her steadfast, and my apology breaks over us
like an egg. I've held her here, she should go
have a rest. She only shrugs: *I'm Italian.*
Everything she is, I'm not. But can see
what I will spend these hours becoming.

I dread a summer to come, the curtain
falling on her stories that held us together:
mothers and fathers, country people bound
to me by a thread, no common blood
but the hours we've stood in labor. How
will I know then what I'm worth?

And how will I stitch this seam for another
wife or child of a child while we move
other mountains, fill kettles in some
kitchen yet to come alive; how will I stand
holding my bones in a careful stack, skull over
spine, knees over ankles, a body well over

all its own secrets of birth and desire;
how will I slip an apron onto that
hipless atelier, take up the knife and give
myself to the sacraments of a household
now unknown to me. How do I know
I will.

Creation Stories

The Christmas she was five, I stayed up
until first light making boots, of all things,
the very pair the brave girl wore
in her storybook. She wanted no other thing.

Leather and needle-punctured
palms, inventing skills I didn't have,
cuffing and embroidering, cursing
an illustrator whose tools were ink
and fancy while I had rawhide:
well, *that* was the year of the boots
worn everywhere but bath and bed.
A story made real. The year she believed
in Santa Claus, she said, *Because
no regular person could do that.*

Years later, she longed for the jacket
all the cool girls had. My ways and means
couldn't stitch that one together. I hoped
a luxury denied might be the travail
a brave girl pressed in her memory book,
instead of the rest: my long-held breath
for those years we had to go it alone
without support, the miles from family,
the making of her everything in the place
where life had nailed us down to nothing.

Now she is a mother herself.
No regular person. She knows the work
of a life is the making of things a child will
not believe we could have made. *Because.*

Meadowview Elementary Spelling Bee

The first graders fall
in a slow, rolling wave
as if before a firing squad,
the first full row swept empty:
brave-enough soldiers but new
to the business of books, they are
cannon fodder for *beam* and *prowl*.

The second graders behind them
stand frozen before the artillery,
hopeless when the *time* comes
and he tries to slip through the
gates as *Tim*. And *easier*, alas,
never in this world so hard.

A sole third grader survives,
stammering through *comrade*
as all of her mates fall away.

The fourth graders quake,
their squadron unequipped
for *siege* or *attrition*. They fall
to *stealth*, survive by *guile*
but are no match for *ingenuous*.

In the end it comes down
to the *proletariat* facing off
appropriation, no surprise—
but I am on tenterhooks for one
small laborer in this camp, word-smitten
since the days before her milk teeth:

She claims her trophy, ecstatic with *glossolalia*.

Blow Me—

away. Like the globe of
dandelion haze on the stalk I put
in your hand the first time you stand
up by yourself in the grass.

down. Like a hurricane
shredding the roof I only want
to keep in one piece over your head-
strong adolescence.

over. Likely as not I am
already stepping aside, blinking
at your improvised inheritance,
feat beyond replication.

out. Like the candle
that lit your way into this dark house
ablaze now with your occupancy. Our bond,
the same as our breathing, out and
in.

After

The morning of the shattered leg
began as a small adventure with my children:
our maritime campaign of languid
tide pools, hardscrabble crabs, slippery rocks,

translucent fish darting wild from our shade
as we wreaked our careless catastrophes,
poking fingers into pink anemones just to see
them curl up into fists of composed trepidation.

After the slick sudden shock, dull crack
of bone collapsing inside its case
of flesh; after the slow crawl back
through the first months of my mending

we curl on the bed, my youngest and I,
reading of runaway bunnies while she
remembers it all again and again. Ocean-eyed
she asks what I will be able to do after this:

Will we skate on the ice next winter? Will I
ever again be the mama who held her tight
on the sled and howled with her when the world
was a fast blue whistle? Yes?

I say yes. I pretend my courage has tentacles
that still reach for light as they did before, *before*
careless chance took its poke at me. Say yes, but feel
curling tight in my chest the anemone of *after*.

Walking Each Other Home

My friend lives on this road
the same as me, two hollows down,
two gladed mountainsides,

briar patches that go without saying,
fields in pumpkin or hay or fallow.
Once, we can never forget, a bear.

And once for too long a season
a road-killed deer whose return to dust
we both watched, the ragged pelt

dried to leather, the shipwreck of rib cage.
My friend alone saw the bear, and
told me of it, the winter of her chemo.

I was the one to see the deer
fresh struck, and had to find words,
though even now I can hardly bear

to say how I watched hooves beating air,
reaching for some blind heaven.
Between us, we know this map by heart.

I walk from my house to hers
and then together we speak of things—
or don't, we are often quiet—

all the way back home to mine. Or she
walks here first, collects me for her return.
Either way, this is the road where we live.

Always we walk each other home.
And always we walk some of it alone.

5

•••••

Dancing with the Devil

Thief

I read Dickens by dim lamplight
casing the joint for plots. This
will not be a holdup, no clearing
out whole cash drawers into my bag—
just a shoplifter's itch: I'll take
the convict benefactor, the woman
who knits rebellions, into my pockets.

Woolf, I read in my room
behind a locked door where she
commands me to empty out everything
like airport security: Nothing!
Walk naked through the passage,
but quick as life I swipe her
badge, make off with her authority.

Emerson, Shelley, Dylan Thomas, H.D.
I read with my face
planted, belly to earth,
leavings of the infinite
composting in my rib cage
sun and rain on my back
bringing up a pelt of new grass.

Dancing with the Devil:
Advice for the Female Poet

Remember about being quiet.
Canny, rowdy, quick, hitting
any nail in the vicinity of its head:
these could be the death of you.
Observing all posted speed limits:
that could be the death of you.

When the choice is speak now
or forever hold your peace,
remember how "peace" comes around
in time to feeling like this crocodile
you are trying to drown.

Remember bloodletting was medicine
back in the day. And who did it.

Remember to leave a window open,
oven door closed, stones on the ground
not in your pockets. Maybe just one
precious in a fist, or against a hot cheek.

Remember all the openings,
same ones used for pushing out
filth, lullabies, the blues, brand-spanking
life bellowing at both ends? That's
what you get. And in defiance
of all higher rulings ever handed down,
remember who lives longer.

Cage of Heaven

Watching the polar bear in his enclosure,
I am thinking of Emily Dickinson,
her fine feet pacing the floors of her house,
the white dress dragging delicately out
the kitchen door and over the circular paths
of the backyard whose perimeters
she would not leave for decades, to the end.
Forsaking even the church she loved.
The dome of trees in her garden would
have to do. Bobolinks for a church choir.

We are all beasts born to our burdens.
Whether by law or the rifle, sharp crack
of sanity or a spine, enclosure is waiting.
This white bear with his splayed paws
parting the water like heavy drapes
was not plucked from some wild perfect life
but orphaned, borne by trauma into this
or nothing. Maybe hell and heaven are both
an existence within limits: the lesser evil.
Do we not all have the same stones
lining the bottoms of our minds, the same
narrow plank of reason crossing the top
of that chasm, same funeral when it breaks
to send us plunging? I've had my days.

Weeks, even. When I could not bear to leave
the safety of my own trees, my choir of
Carolina wrens. I have what she had: fleets
of ships in our libraries to take us anywhere;
some goodly sort of god arranging his furniture
in our houses, that we might try out heaven;
and poetry's clear pools where the lone swimmer
can feel against bare skin the ice of revelation.

The plank has cracked for this bear
I'm afraid. I watch him and find myself
praying for the saving arts we all have
to make ourselves—that on his circular walks
through blue-painted concrete glaciers
he is meeting angels in hats of snow.
That when he swims and swims he believes
he will find things heretofore unseen—
not the fish at hand but the piercing teeth
of risk, his polar zero at the bone.

Insomniac Villanelle

The chore of blunting night's tormented edges
    Austen, Byron, Cather, Dickens, Emerson
while cats of sentience creep out on the ledges

demands some dull device for driving wedges
    Faulkner, García Márquez, Hugo, Ibsen
into the ticking torment of night's edges

a steady, flogging tedium that fledges
    Joyce, Kazantzakis, Lessing, Merton, Nin
tense flights of apprehension from the hedges,

hounds spirits from the stairs, and slowly dredges
    Orwell, Plath, Queirós, Rilke, Stein
regrets like broken glass from night's deep edges

and still tomorrow's weary pending pledges
    Tolstoy, Updike, Verne, oh patient Whitman
are cats of sentience sprawling on the ledges

    Saint-Exupéry will pass, Yeats, Zola. Austen,
    Jane—you again, Cather, Eliot, no! Byron
this blunt and beaten night has lost its edges.
Now there's birdsong, daylight on the ledges.

My Afternoon with The Postman

The day of the cruel review, I fled
to the museum believing beauty
might cotton the clappers of all these
alarm bells in my head. Beauty failed.
I sat on a bench in the corner with The Postman.

Who knows why they put him in that corner?
The proudly functional blue hat. Beard
like a spring flood. Red-rimmed eyes
unnerving. Or no, disarming. Sympathetic.

Critics are asses, I told him. Why make art
for people who never make anything,
who live only to dismember it and send
its creators to sit in the corner like children?

The Postman appeared content with his position.

But artists, I insisted, we who make ourselves
of self-critical bones, self-critical skin! This is not
some business of rapping us on the knuckles.
This is knowing the peanut allergy
and making the peanut butter sandwich.

The Postman wasn't biting.

I tried gossip, thinking surely every postman
has carried a neighborhood story or two around
in his bag: my critic's squalid habits, his vendetta
against my friends—these nitpickings roused
the interest you'd expect from a dead French mailman.

Fine, then. What kind of mail did you bring Van Gogh?

That did it. *Mostly bills. Tabac, le caviste,*
the regular gathering storm of the landlady,
he was always short of cash. You know. Artists.

So much for my gloomy party. I'm not starving.
I changed the subject: He gave you the eyes of Christ.

Not really. It's a good likeness. Even my wife
thought so. Augustine, now there was a critic.

Really, those are your eyes?

Must be. He couldn't pay anyone else to sit for him,
the girls who smile for a price. The faces he could
afford were sunflowers. He didn't know a soul
when he came to Arles, asking me every day for news
of the locals, even news of their cats, anything
to keep me there on his porch to light a pipe with him.

He made you look like Socrates.

Lonely men mistake kindness for a philosophy.

People think genius thrives in tortured isolation.

Lonelier ones can mistake contempt for kindness.

You're suggesting I'm lucky to know the difference.

For example, that painter friend of his who kept promising
to visit! Vincent wagged his tail like a dog for that man.

Gauguin, we've all heard about that. His tormenter.

I was the one to fetch him from the hospital, after
the incident. I took him for a good dinner.

So I'm asking, was it criticism that did him in?

Critics are flies. They buzz. They vanish, unremembered.

But the hate mail. You would know—did anyone say
he had no business making stars so fierce, or trees
so pointed, the whole thing uncomfortably much
too close to the truth of the mess we're in?

They didn't have to. They just didn't buy his paintings.
No one had to be told not to buy a painting.

It's different now. Critics tell millions of people not
to buy our work, who mostly weren't going to buy it
anyway. The artist risks unending humiliation.

Also unending love, but that is not the point.

I have to ask, then.

Madame, what could I tell you
more than one hundred years after all
the postmen I knew in Arles, all the women,
smiling or otherwise, throwing water on
alley cats, the cats themselves, the stars
and trees such as they were and also of course,
the artist: gone entirely.
Look at you looking into the eyes of a stranger
for the consolation of his quiet ear.

6

·····

Where It Begins

Where It Begins

Winter is for women—The woman, still at her knitting . . .
The bees are flying. They taste the spring.

—SYLVIA PLATH

It all starts with the weather. Comes a day when summer
gives in to the slenderest freshet of chill, and just like that,
you're gone. Wild in love with the autumn proviso. Trees
will light themselves ember-orange at the hemline, starting
their ritual drama of self-immolation. The honkling chain
gang of geese overhead fleeing warmward-ho, chuckling
over their big escape, you see it all. But you will stick it out.
Through the woodsmoke season that opens all hearts' doors
into kitchen industry and soup on the stove, the signs wink
at you from everywhere: sticks of kindling, brushstrokes of
snow on branches—this is the whole world calling you to
take up your paired swords against the coming freeze. The
chromosomes plied by all your thin-skinned forebears can
offer no more bottomless thrill than the point-nosed plow
of preparedness. It begins on the morning you see your
children's bare feet swinging under the table while they
eat cold bowls of cereal. You shudder like a dog hauling up
from the lake, but can't throw off the pall of those little
pink-palmy feet. You will swaddle your children in wool.

It starts with a craving to fill the long evening downslant.
There will be whole days of watching winter drag her skirts
across the mud-yard from east to west, going nowhere. You
will want to pin down these wadded handfuls of time, to
frame them on a 24-stitch gauge. Ten to the inch, ten rows to
the hour, straggling trellises of days held fast in the acreage
of a shawl. Time by this means is domesticated and cannot

run away. You pick up sticks because Time is just asking for it, already lost before it arrives. The frightful movie your family has chosen for Friday night, for instance. They insist it will be watched, so with just the one lamp turned on at the end of the sofa you can be there too, keeping your hands busy and your eyeshades half drawn; yes, people will be murdered, cars will be wrecked, and you will come through in one piece, plus a pair of mittens. It's the same everywhere. Your river is rife with doldrums and eddies: the waiting room, the plane, the train, the lecture, the meeting. Oh, sweet mother of Christ, the meeting. The-PTA-the-town-council-the-school-board-the-bored-board, interminably haggled items of the agenda. Your feet want to run for their lives but your fingers know to dig in the bag and unsheathe their handy stays against impatience, the smooth paired oars, sturdy lifeboat of yarn. This meeting may bottom-drag and list on its keel, stranded in the Sargasso Sea of Agenda, and you alone will sail away on your thrifty raft of unwasted time. You alone, to swaddle the world in wool.

Strangely, it also begins with the opposite: a hankering to lose time. To banish all possibilities: the shattered day undone, the bitter tea leaves of old regard, the words forever pushing ahead of each other in line, queuing up to be written. Especially those. Words that drub, drub at the skull's concave inner wall. Words that are birds in a linear flock, pelting themselves all night long against the windowpane. Nothing can stop the words but this mute alphabet of knit and purl. The curl of your cupped hand scoops up long drinks of calm. The rhythm is from down inside, rocking cradle, heartbeat, ocean. Waves on a rockless shore.

Sometimes it starts terribly. With the injury or the accident, a wrecked life flung down like an armload of broken chair legs on your doorstep. Here lies the recuperation, whose miles you

can't see across, let alone traverse. Chasm of woe uncrossable
by any bridge, here lies you. And in comes the friend bearing
needles of pale bamboo—twin shafts of light!—and ombré
skeins in shades that march through the stages of grief, burnt
umber to gold to dandelion. She is not in a listening mood, the
friend. Today she commands you to make something of all this.
And to your broken heart's surprise, you do.

It begins with a circle of friends. Always there is something
beyond your beyond, the aged parents and teenager who crack
up the family cars on the same day. There is the bone-picked
divorce, the winter of chemo, the gorgeous mistake, the long
unraveling misery that needs company, reading glasses and
glasses of wine and all the chairs pulled into the living room.
Cast on, knit two together girlfriendwise. Pick up the pieces
where you can, along the headless yoke or scandalously loose
button placket. Knitting makes the talk go softer, as long as it
needs to be. Laughter makes dropped stitches.

It begins with a pattern. The riveting twist of a cable, a spiral,
a ladder, eyes of the lynx, traveling vines. A pattern hallooing
to you from your neighbor's sweater when you're only trying
for small talk, distracting you until sheepishly you stop and
ask permission to memorize the lay of her sweater's land. Once
it starts, there's no stopping. In your sturdy frame of double-
pointed needles you cultivate the apical stem of sock-sleeve-
stocking-cap. From a seed of pattern everything grows: xylem
and phloem of ribs, a trunk with branches of sleeves, the skirt
that bells daffodilwise. You are god of this wild botany. You
may take the familiar map in hand, look it over with all best
intentions, then throw it away and head for uncharted waters
where there be monsters. There you'll discover a promised land
of garments previously undevised: gloves for the extra long of

hand, or short, or the firecracker nephew with one digit missing in action. Sweaters for the short-waisted, the broad-shouldered, your best beloveds all covetous of the bespoke, looking to you for the bliss of a perfect fit.

And a perfect color. It starts there too. An eye has hungers of its own: the particular green of leaves overturned by the oncoming storm. A desert's russet bronze, mustard of Appalachian spring, some spectral intangible you long to possess. Or a texture. There are nowhere near enough words for this. Textures have family trees: cloud and thistledown are cousin to catpelt and infantscalp and earlobe. Petal is a texture, and lime peel and nettle and five o'clock shadow and sandstone and soap and slither. Drape is the child of loft and crimp; wool is a stalwart crone who remembers everything, while emptyhead white-haired cotton forgets. And in spite of their disparate natures, these strings can be lured to sit down together and play a fiber concerto whole in the cloth. A lamb's virgin fleece can be spun with the fuzz of a lush blue hare or a twist of flax, you name it, silkworm floss or twiny bamboo. Creatures not known to converse in nature can be introduced and married on the spot. The spindle is your altar; you are the matchmaker, steady on the treadle, fingers plying animal with vegetable, devising your new, surprisingly peaceable kingdoms. Fingers can read; they have secret libraries and illicit affairs. Twined into the fleece of a ewe on shearing day, hands can read the history of her winter: how many snows, how barren or sweet her mangers. For best results stand in the pasture and throw your arms around her.

Because really it starts there, in the barn on shearing day, with the circle of friends assembled. One fleece shorn all of a piece, flung out on a table surrounded by help at the ready. All hands point toward the center like an introverted clock, the better for combing the fleece. Fingers can see in the dark to pull out twigs and cockleburs. Fleeces rolled and stacked look for all the world like loaves of bread on a bakery shelf, or sheaves of grain or any other money in the bank: the universal currency of a planet where people get cold. On shearing day all ledgers will be balanced; the sheep are woolly by morning and naked by night, as barrows fill and warmth is bankrolled in futures. Six women can skirt a fleece in ten minutes, just enough time to run and collect the next, if the shearer is handy. It starts early, this day, and goes long.

It starts in the barn every morning of the year. The sheep are both eager and wary at the sight of you, the bringer of hay, reaper of wool, as you enter the barn for the daily accounts. You inhale the florid scents of sweet feed and mineral urine, and there they stand eyeing you every time, on blizzard nights or mornings of spring lambing when you hurry out at dawn to find dumbfounded mothers of twins licking their wispy trembling slips of children, exhorting them to look alive. The sloe-eyed flock mistrusts you fundamentally, but still they come running when you shake the exquisite bucket of grain, money that talks to yearlings and chary wethers alike, loudest of all to the ravenous barrel-round pregnant ewes that gallop home with udders tolling like church bells. In all weather you take their measure and send them out to pasture again. Willingly they return to their posts with their gentle gear-grinding jaws, their wool thickening on winter's advance, beginning your sweater for you at the true starting gate.

Everything starts, of course, with the sheep and the grass. Under her greening scalp the earth frets and dreams and knits her issue. Between her breasts, on hillsides too steep for the plow, the sheep place little sharp feet on invisible paths and lead their curly-haired sons and daughters out onto the tart green blades of eternal breakfast. It starts on tumbled-up lambspring mornings when you slide open the heavy barn door and expel the pronking gambol of newborn wildhooray into daylight. And in summer's haze when they scramble up on boulders to scan the horizon with eyes made to fit just-so, horizontal eyes, flattened to that shape by distant skulking predators avoided for all time. And in the gloaming, when the ewes high up on the pasture raise their heads suddenly at the sight of you, conceding to come down as a throng in their rockinghorse gait, surrendering under dog-press to the barn-tendered mercy of nightfall.

It starts where everything starts. With muffleblind snows and dingle springs, the singular pursuit of cud, the fibrous alchemy of a herd spinning grass into wool. This is all your business. Hands plunged into a froth of yarn are as helpless as hands thrust into a lover's hair, for they are divining the grass-pelt life of everything: the world. Sunshine, heavenly photosynthetic host, sweet leaves of grass all singing the fingers electric that tingle to brace the winter, charged by the plied double helices of all creatures that have prepared and survived on the firmament of patience and swaddled children. It's all of a piece, knitting. All one thing.

7

•••••

The Nature of Objects

Ghost Pipes

Not fungi. Ethereal flowers, the slim stem piping
up through scale of leaf, the downturned bell,
all perfectly white. Not cream or pearl. Translucent
jewel of ice gleaming from the toes of a forest.

Once this plant was ordinary heath. Then came
the day it renounced the safety of photosynthesis.
Turned away from the sun's daily bread for a riskier
life, tapping deep strata to drink from tree roots,
pulling their blessed sugars straight from darkness.

Disparage the scroungers all you please. This flower
is my darling. Imagine, forsaking chlorophyll.
In my own time I have walked clean away
from numbing shelter, marriage, the steady paycheck,
taking my own wild chance on the freelance life.

And when I walk among ghost pipes, their little
spectral music in the dark wood quickens my heart:
song of a moment, the risky road *yes* taken
to desire, escape. The day that changed everything.

The Nature of Objects

Contained in the valley of my hand
a wilderness of feathers the colors of ash, moss,
daylight, chalk, weightless compendium
of skull and bones, toes curled to no branch
ever again. A thump on my kitchen window:
Orange-crowned Warbler.

Dead, that's what we'll call it. Alive
it was song, migration, eggshell strength,
brittle tundra, a mind for deriving
equations of polar magnets and equinox
that would collapse my big, slow brain.
Knowing exactly the day for leaving
needle spruce ice, for casting its lot in a river
of air, down through the hourglass waist
of the Americas to seek an insect fortune
in the broad-leaved promised land—
but here instead. Stopped by the fatal
invisible barrier of my construction.

John James Audubon, illustrious portraitist
of nature, shot birds by the thousands,
having in his time no other way to see them
perfectly. This was the common practice.
Every species described by art or science,
every name, assigned to a dead bird.

Still life, *nature morte*: the legacy is a book
of names all wrong for the living. Quick
punctuation marks revising stanzas of leaf,
a voice inclined to a mate's perfect pitch:
the living can very well name themselves,
have nothing they need to surrender to

an earthbound mammal's eye. Only by taking
the bird in hand may any of us see
—the hint of Orange in the warbler's Crown
—the vireo's faint Black Whisker
—the woodpecker's discreetly Red Belly
terms incidentally meaningless in birdsong.

The things a person will murder in order to name.
A nature of objects, construction of human
marvel, Nature itself—a place
to go visit, collect some particular plenty,
and then come home again—there you have it:
the spectacular lie of our species.

The truth is unbearable.
The pane of glass holds nothing inside.
Or out—no study of field marks and plumage
can classify life in the kingdom without
the corridor connecting florescence
and rain to ice and spruce, the borealis,
the forest of scent trails, the buckshot
notwithstanding, the bear sizing up the man
and deciding to amble away, or not:
the unspeakable confederacy of equals.

The truth is this wren at daybreak
mocking all the windows of my house,
announcing his ownership of my yard
in a language that has no word for my kind.
It's singing oneself awake like that—
and just like that, the song gone quiet—
that calls me out on the glazed face
of the deadly barrier, nothing but reflection.

Come August, a Seven-Day Rain

In May we planted our crops in mud,
accepting the false testament of plenty, saying
nothing of the deficit that had persisted for
the last three years, slight enough but held over,

the checkbook not quite balanced
against the foreseeable disaster.

June brought the green beetles out
to hum their heathen hallelujahs, raiding
our waterless larders leaf and vein. And if
a stranger to this country remarked on the green
of our cornfields, we did not point out

the parched-silt color of death
edging the leaves of the tallest trees
and the riven floors of our wells.

July cicadas keened to a hard star-punctured sky,
cucumbers folded leaves over their stillborn young,
beetles dried to rusks on the vines they defeated,
cattle lowered their heads in whitened pastures

of the church of all things
and as one, we prayed.
There is only one god
and its name is this. Now.

Ephemera

And the equinox said let there be light
on this moment of sun-warmed forest floor
from this open eyeblink of sky before
the leaves of the naked timberland unfurl
and cast their darkness across the land:
let there be bloodroot,
birthroot, hepatica, coltsfoot,
wake robin, adder's tongue,
Solomon's seal, Jack in his pulpit,
Dutchman's breeches,
let there be an orgy of anther and ovary.
And on the second day the winged things
came unto them, the solitary bees
and yellowjackets,
the lumbering ground beetles
and the bee fly *Bombylius major*
and the lips were touched with pollen
and it was good.
On the days thereafter the petals looked down
and covered their sex,
rolled their seeds unto the earth,
for thus their world is made.
And the small leaves withered to sleep by dusk
and were not seen again for the long
three hundred sixty days of a wildflower night.

Love Poem, with Birds

They are your other flame. Your world
begins and ends with the dawn chorus,
a plaint of saw-whet owl, and in between,
the seven different neotropical warblers
you will see on your walk to the mailbox.
It takes a while. I know now not to worry.

Once I resented your wandering eye that
flew away mid-sentence, chasing any raft
of swallows. I knew, as we sat on the porch
unwinding the cares of our days, you were
listening to me through a fine mesh of oriole,
towhee, flycatcher. I said it was like kissing
through a screen door: *You're not all here.*

But who could be more present than a man
with the patience of sycamores, showing me
the hummingbird's nest you've spied so high
in a tree, my mortal eye can barely make out
the lichen-dabbed knot on an elbow of branch.
You will know the day her nestlings leave it.

The wonder is that such an eye, that lets not
even the smallest sparrow fall from notice,
beholds me also. That I might walk the currents
of our days with red and golden feathers
in my hair, my plain tongue laced with music.
That we, the birds and I, may be text and
illumination in your book of common prayer.

Swimming in the Wamba

A man cannot step in the same river twice.
—HERACLITUS

But yes, after all, here is the river where crocodiles
bellied in shallows and I also bellied like that,
half-eyed above the cold breach and half below
in a child's needy gambol with thrill and dread.

And among all the wily forgotten tastes, nsafou
fruits and green saka-saka, here are the palm nuts
I pulled through my teeth to suck their marrow of fat
for a body yearning, running from day to dark with
no milk or meat, the humming of that special hunger.

The crocodiles are gone now, shot from canoes
by men who know the endless incaution of children,
and these palm nuts answer no animal question
for a body that hasn't gone to sleep hungry in years.

Still, when I come home to Africa, this happens:
I pull red palm nut gristle through my teeth,
I belly in the river with watch-ticked eyes,
I am small in love with just this fear, this hunger.
And this cold current was always exactly here.

Cradle

On a forest path steamed
with the scent of elephant urine
leading to pink-tusked daylight,
primate eyes take measure
of the audacious hominid passage,
relatives who no longer speak to me
looking down from the limbs
of the fathers. This morning of
the world, deliver me from darkness
into savanna. I will walk upright
hands-first, to spare my eyes
from the knife-edged grasses,
from the pitiless buffalo stare,
from the river of tsetse flies that
rush from bloodtank to bloodtank
delivering parasite parcels exactly
as old as humankind, honed
through all the time in the world
to strike me down perfectly. Make no
mistake: we are all in this together.

Here is the ground for forgetting all
the deadbolted hiding places
where survival masquerades as
the purchased fit of a tailored suit:
the paycheck a man believes he's earned.
All fool's gold next to the payout
delivered at birth through a
narrow canal: an upright bearing,
opposable thumb, clever braincase—
the plunder he owns without asking.

Here is primacy laid bare and
trembling on a path through unquiet
forest and longtooth grass. Here
even the blood-charged insects roar,
demanding allegiance to all the
ancient enemies that make the man—
have winnowed me right out
through a billion genomic
crossroads toward some other eye
that might have been, some other
unlucky shape left for dead—oh, I
could fall down on this
road to my own Damascus,
blinded by the stupid luck of the matter:
Survival, quicksilver reckoning
scooped by chance from a swamp of loss.
The undeserved inheritance.

Down Under

Our boots hit the flint trail
striking sparks of wonder
at the choice we get: here
of all places. Foreigners
to this red-desert eucalypt
marsupial underworld, not one
single familiar. Twenty wide-
eyed miles today or bust.

Whittled down to mallee, the trees
retract their shade to islands.
Each one claimed by a roo
and her joey, elbows on knees,
eyes dark marbles of judgment:
what fool creatures are we,
to work so hard in broad daylight
with nothing after us.

The water in our bottles
grows hot as weak tea, then
scarce. We become nothing
but our thirst.
Become our body
temperatures poised on the ledge
of the one small window
a mammal is allowed.

Heartbeat is the telegram
to believe: full stop.
Elbows on knees we crouch down
under scrub for shade, familiar
territory, hands to sand,
roots to moisture.
Join the tribe of creatures
getting out of here alive.

The Hands of Trees

Maple is wide open, splay-fingered
in joy—jazz hands. Or the friendly gesture,
making a point politely. As if Canadian.

Catalpa, a churchful of Southern Baptist ladies
in summer dresses. Devoutly moist, mid-sermon,
held in suspense as Jesus rounds up his
rascal lambs: the steady motion of all those fans.

Aspen, notorious for the palsy.
To be fair, the air is thin up there
in the Rockies. And sometimes, wolves.

Sassafras wears mittens knitted by
a harebrained aunt: sometimes with an extra
thumb, sometimes none whatsoever.

Fig leaves, cupped as if to conceal—as
everyone and his brother knows by now—
the shy parts of Eve. Less delicate than you
might think: sturdily veined, made for the job.

Redbud, Southern belle—all heart,
no backbone—thrusts hers forward, dangling
limp from the wrist. Waiting to be kissed.

Mimosa, anyone can see: how they tremble with thanks
for a star that concedes to work the day shift;
how they reach for light's full octave,
recoil from a firm handshake,
long to stroke the velvet nap of night, but with dusk's
owl eyes blinking open, press closed in prayer.

Mussel, Minnow

Fatmucket, Snuffbox, Wartyback, which
among these bivalves stuck for life
in creekpebble bottom could wrest much
notice from the spiny higher-minded—
we who hitch our wagons to stars?

What of Heelsplitter, Plain Pocketbook,
Higgins Eye Pearly, just so many peasants'
plow blades dug into their own mucky turf?
A mussel's hopes are small, it would seem,
and all downstream from here. But look:

This is life wide and strange upon the earth
where even the lower orders have tricks
up a sleeve. In this case her own mussel flesh
encased in shell, but now coquettishly exposed
in a minnow shape, with false eye and fin.

Or arranged as crayfish appendages, dangling
claws, jerky gait. Or a glutinous fishing line with
a lure at its end. Each of these gifts, a Trojan horse
devised to tempt the large-mouthed fish
to cruise in close for a bite, or for urgent love—

and get instead in its startled fish-face
a milky blast of a thousand mussel children.
With tiny claws they grasp gills, sip blood, catch
a ride upstream. Then drop and settle on clear
cold pebbled pastures, stuff of molluscan ambition.

One could pity the fish, our protean kin,
the nerve and backbone and brainy upward
mobility of it all. But in the countinghouse
of the higher mind and its endless debts to desire,
my money's on the literally brainless mussel.

Matabele

Matabele ants,
named for a warrior tribe
alleged to be the cruelest,
go marching nightwise
launching their quotidian
genocide on their neighbors
the termites whose only
job is to inherit the earth.

Meekly they wait,
eating their lot of soil
to improve its nature.
Pitilessly they come,
the raiding warriors
six hundred strong
storming the chambers,
crushing pale bodies
to carry off for fodder
but always stopping
short of the full execution.
They leave the queen alive.

The Victorians wrote of
Nature red in tooth and claw,
knowing not the half of it:
still undiscovered, the likes
of the disciplined Matabele
ants that spare the crown;
or the civil virus houseguest
that visits for five days
and then departs before
its sniffling host succumbs.
Nature is nothing if not
a congress of partial kindness.

And who is to say
where cruelty and mercy
may lie down together
to make their mottled children?

In the sickbed from which
the newly hale will rise
and go forth to shed
the seeds of their affliction.
In the throbbing abdomen
of one queen alone
in her darkness, pulsing
eggs, beginning again
the rearing of future
fodder, attuned to a rogue
vibration, listening
for the barbarians at the gate.

Great Barrier

The cathedral is burning. Absent flame or smoke,
stained glass explodes in silence, fractal scales
of angel damsel rainbow parrot. Charred beams
of blackened coral lie in heaps on the sacred floor,
white stones fallen from high places, spires collapsed,
crushing the sainted turtle and gargoyle octopus.

Something there is in my kind that cannot love
a reef, a tundra, a plain stone breast of desert, ever
quite enough. A tree perhaps, once recomposed
as splendid furniture. A forest after the whole of it
is planed to posts and beams and raised to a heaven
of earnest construction in the name of Our Lady.

All Paris stood on the bridges to watch her burning,
believing a thing this old, this large and beautiful,
must be holy and cannot be lost. And coral temples
older than Charlemagne suffocate unattended,
bleach and bleed from the eye, the centered heart.

Lord of leaves and fishes, lead me across this great divide.
Teach me how to love the sacred places, not as one
devotes to One who made me in his image and is bound
to love me back. I mean as a body loves its microbial skin,
the worm its nape of loam, all secret otherness forgiven.

Love beyond anything I will ever make of it.

Forests of Antarctica

From here the oldest trees will speak
to one another in the oldest language,
chemical breath, touch in darkness,
rootlets seeking rootlets holding
hands underground for succor. And I
could pass among them hearing nothing.
Or I could pause on the tilted light
of slate-scrabbled path in a silence
of moss and try to fathom their stillness:

How nothing stirs their hearts.
How patience is a promise a seed makes
to its ground, from the day of cracking
and rooting in, clinging to this escarpment
since before the trial of Socrates, before
the tilting up of plinths at Stonehenge.
Already ringed with moss and age
when Jesus walked out of Nazareth.
Betrothal of these giants to their place
has left them crouched on buttressed trunks
high above the ground, leg-roots exposed
by all the rains that have washed the earth
out from under them since the beginning.

Everything has already happened here.
Still the ancient beeches hold their ground
with moss-knuckled toes, remembering
a Gondwanaland of their youth when
faraway Antarctica was yet a forested nation.
Standing shoulder to shoulder they braced
for the breaking apart of the known,
a rumbling violence of stones, mountain
dashed against mountain, two ships parting.

The trees exhaled in communion, rode their
new continents, survived the end of one world.

In the Great Dividing Range I crave to repent.
In filtered tree fern light I confess the sins
of my tribe: we worship the future, demean
the past, pay no mind to the present.
But a future, cut off from the promise of ever
joining history, lies already dead on its altar
while we chew on our restless feet.

What's to become of our own seeds
and betrothals: all these floss-haired children
inside us that want to live? Want to move,
stay, eat the soil from under the house,
move on. Want to hold fast but cannot
hold still. I am lifting them up
as newborns to the nursery window
looking out on the forests of Antarctica.
I tell them: *This is your home.*
Tell them: *None of this is yours.*
Do not believe as I did. When
the world breaks open, fall apart
with her entrails, fall with the stones or fly.
Let the crush of it make you into some
new thing not yourself. See how these trees
take the teat of the world and suckle it,
drinking time, knowing it is perfect
with or without them. Lacking their religion,
you will have to make your own.

You are the world that stirs. This is the world that waits.

NOTES

"How to Fly" borrows an image—the unbodied breath of a bird—from Percy Bysshe Shelley's "To a Skylark."

"How to Survive This" was published in the *New York Times* Magazine, March 26, 2020.

"How to Be Married" is for Rob and Paula Kingsolver.

"How to Love Your Neighbor" is for Frances Goldin.

"How to Be Hopeful," part of the Duke University commencement address, May 2009, was published in *Creating a Life You'll Love*, edited by Mark Chimsky-Lustig (Sellers Publishing, 2009).

The cycle *Pellegrinaggio* is dedicated *con tanto amore* to Joann Hopp, who was born (and, frankly, remains) Giovanna Spano.

"This Is How They Come Back to Us" owes its title and spirit to Wendell Berry. The poems in this section are for the dead who are named and the living who bear their losses, especially Anna and Clara Petri, Sara Hopp, Joann Hopp, and Joe Findley.

For "My Mother's Last Forty Minutes" I'm indebted to my sister, brother, and father, custodians of their own versions of this story, with a nod to William Carlos Williams's "XXII" from *Spring and All*.

The italicized lines in "My First Derby Party" are from the song "My Old Kentucky Home," by Stephen Foster. The poem is dedicated to Fenton Johnson.

"Creation Stories," "Meadowview Elementary Spelling Bee," "Blow Me—," and "After" are for Camille and Lily Kingsolver.

The title "Walking Each Other Home" acknowledges accidental similarity to a quote from Ram Dass, "We are always walking each other home." The poem is dedicated to Felicia Mitchell.

"Cage of Heaven" borrows images and lines from these poems by Emily Dickinson: "Some keep the Sabbath going to church," "I felt a Funeral in my brain," "Who has not found the heaven below," "To fight aloud is very brave," and "A narrow fellow in the grass."

"Insomniac Villanelle" is for my three A.M. friends, with thanks to Sally Carpenter.

"My Afternoon with The Postman" describes Vincent van Gogh's portraits of his mail carrier, Joseph Roulin, with thanks to the Barnes Foundation gallery in Philadelphia, where one of these masterpieces hangs unobtrusively in a corner.

"Where It Begins" was previously published in slightly different form in *Knitting Yarns*, edited by Ann Hood (W. W. Norton, 2014); and *The Best American Science and Nature Writing 2014*, edited by Deborah Blum and Tim Folger (Houghton Mifflin, 2014). The epigraph is from Sylvia Plath's poem "Wintering."

"Ghost Pipes" was published in *Orion*, Autumn 2020. Ghost Pipes are *Monotropa uniflora* (also known as corpse plant or Indian pipe), found in woodlands of North America, European Russia, and Asia. The freelance life is never simple.

"Ephemera" is dedicated to the staff and friends of the Blue Ridge Discovery Center in Konnarock, Virginia.

"Love Poem, with Birds" is for Steven Hopp.

"Cradle" is dedicated to Alicia Paghera.

"Mussel, Minnow" lists a few of many deceptions used by American freshwater mussels for the transport of their larvae; for an overview, see "How Mussels Fool Fish into Carrying Their Parasitic Babies," by Jason Bittel, in *National Geographic*, November 28, 2017.

"Great Barrier" was published in *Time* magazine, September 12, 2019.

One of its lines echoes the opening of "Mending Wall" by Robert Frost: "Something there is that doesn't love a wall."

"Forests of Antarctica" gratefully acknowledges inspiration from the lines "I am the earth that waits. / You are the earth that walks," from "What the Trail Says," by Pamela Alexander, in *Slow Fire*. The referenced trees are Antarctic beeches (*Nothofagus moorei*) in the Great Dividing Range of Australia, part of the relict Gondwana Rainforest that once dominated Antarctica. They became Australian flora when the two continents separated 180 million years ago. Individual trees on Mount Bithongabel are 2,500 to 3,000 years old, with some cloned groupings estimated to be as old as 15,000 years.

ABOUT THE AUTHOR

BARBARA KINGSOLVER's books of fiction, poetry, and creative nonfiction are widely translated and have won numerous literary awards. She is the founder of the PEN/Bellwether Prize, and in 2000 was awarded the National Humanities Medal, the country's highest honor for service through the arts. Prior to her writing career she studied and worked as a biologist. She lives with her husband on a farm in southern Appalachia.

HarperCollins books may be purchased for educational, business, or sales promotional use. For information, please email the Special Markets Department at SPsales@harpercollins.com.

Originally published as *How to Fly* in Great Britain in 2020 by Faber and Faber.

FIRST EDITION

Designed by Leah Carlson-Stanisic

Library of Congress Cataloging-in-Publication Data has been applied for.

ISBN 978-0-06-299308-3

20 21 22 23 24 LSC 10 9 8 7 6 5 4 3 2 1